Building a Sencha Touch Application

A Hands-On Tutorial for Mobile Application Developers

Book Version: 2.4.0

Copyright © MiamiCoder.com

www.miamicoder.com

Table of contents

About This Book

How this book will help you

The goal of this book is to teach you how to create a Sencha Touch 2 application. If you are new to Sencha Touch, or are already familiar with the Framework but have not built an entire application by yourself, this is a great book for you.

In the process of building an application, you will learn the following topics:

- The building blocks of a Sencha Touch application.
- How to implement the Model-View-Controller pattern in a Sencha Touch application.
- How to create an application with multiple views, and how to implement an intuitive navigation pattern between them.
- How to create list-based and master-detail user interfaces in a Sencha Touch application.
- How to capture, edit and validate data using Sencha Touch form-based user interfaces.
- How Sencha Touch stores data on the device using HTML5 local storage.
- How to create a production build of your application.

This book is an excellent way to get started with Sencha Touch because it will teach you the Framework's main concepts through practice. After you read it, you will feel confident that you can develop great Sencha Touch applications.

About warranties and trademarks

The information in this book is distributed on an "as is" basis, without warranty. Although every precaution has been taken in the preparation of this work, neither I nor my employers shall have any liability to any person or entity with respect to any loss or damage caused or alleged to be caused directly or indirectly by the information contained in this work.

Trademarked names may appear in this book. Rather than use a trademark symbol with every occurrence of a trademarked name, I use the names only in an editorial fashion and to the benefit of the trademark owner, with no intention of infringement of the trademark.

Chapter 1: Introducing the Notes App

What you will learn in this chapter

The Sencha Touch application you will build in this book allows its users to take notes and store them on the device running the app. We will call the application the Notes app.

These are your goals for this chapter:

- Define the app's features.
- Design the app's main views.
- Learn how a Sencha Touch Application works.
- Learn how to organize a Sencha Touch application's directories and files for an optimal development experience.

Just so you have an idea of how the app will look after you build it, here are a couple of screenshots of the finished Notes app:

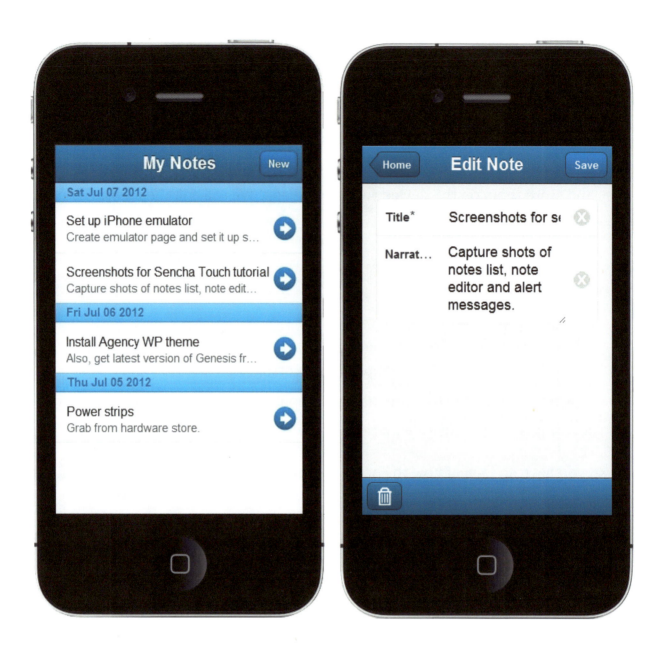

The features of the Notes app

The Notes application has a simple feature set. You want to give your customers five basic abilities:

1. Create notes.
2. Edit notes.
3. Delete notes.

4. View the entire collection of notes.
5. Store notes on the device that is running the application, across browser sessions.

Before you start implementing these features, we are going to take a few minutes to talk about the building blocks of a Sencha Touch application.

What is a Sencha Touch application?

In general, a Sencha Touch application will consist of one or more views, one or more data models and stores, and one or more controllers.

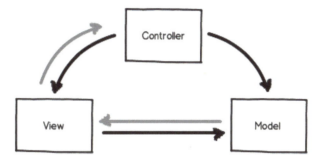

Views

Views have a dual role; they render representations of the data in the models, and capture and transmit user input to the controllers. You can build views using Sencha Touch visual components such as containers, panels, form panels and toolbars.

Controllers

Controllers translate the user's input into changes in the data and/or the behavior of the application. Sencha Touch controllers have built-in features that allow them to listen to events generated within the views and other parts of the application, and perform actions based on these events. These actions might include modifying the data the application stores, generating requests to the server, and activating and deactivating views.

Models

Models and stores represent the application's data and state. They work together to keep the application's data in a correct and safe state, and provide means to send data to the server or to on-device databases.

Profiles

With the variety of mobile devices out there, it is important that mobile applications provide the best experience possible for each device. A Sencha Touch application can also contain a number of classes where you define the supported devices, and what stores, models, views and controllers will work for each device. These classes are called Device Profiles.

The Application

Logically, you can think of a Sencha Touch Application as a number of views, controllers, models, stores and profiles that work together to perform a number of functions that collectively form the application's features:

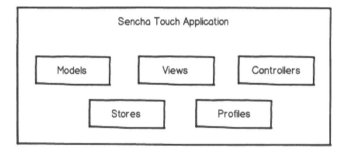

The first area you will work on is the views.

Designing the NotesList view

The Notes app needs a view that will render the list of the notes that the app has saved on the device. The NotesList view will be the main view of the application. Users will first see this view when they launch the app.

This is a mock-up of the NotesList view:

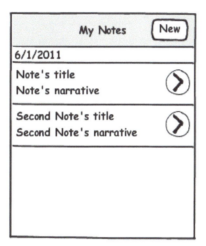

When modeling a user interface, particularly when we are getting started with a Framework like Sencha Touch, most of us struggle with how to map the mock-up elements to the Framework's native widgets and components. As depicted below, the NotesList view is an *Ext.Container* component that hosts a *TitleBar* and a *List*:

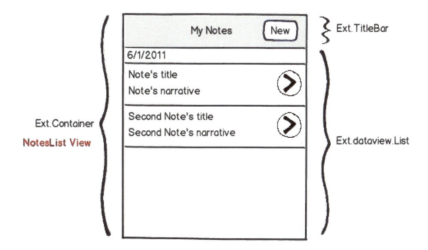

Designing the NoteEditor view

The second view of the app, the NoteEditor view, will allow users to create, edit and delete notes. This view will look just like this mock-up:

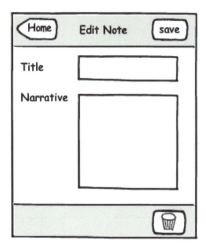

As depicted below, you can build the NoteEditor view using a *FormPanel*, a *TitleBar* and a *Toolbar*:

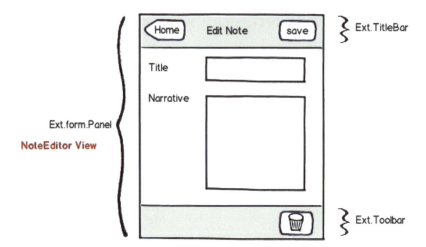

The Viewport

You also need a mechanism for users to navigate back and forth between these screens. As each Sencha Touch Application gets a *Viewport* instance upon launch, you will use the Viewport to take care of rendering the NotesList and NoteEditor views, as well as manage the navigation between them:

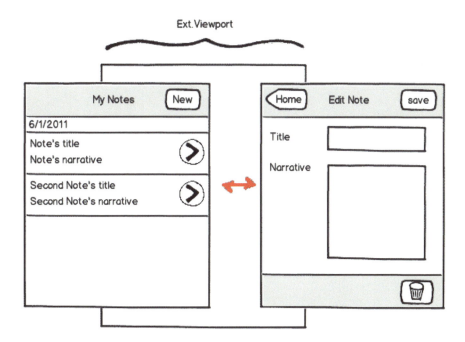

What you need to start developing with Sencha Touch

To develop the application, you need to download the Sencha Touch's SDK, which is available through this link:

http://www.sencha.com/products/touch/download/.

In addition, you need to download the Sencha Command, available through this link: http://www.sencha.com/products/sencha-cmd/download. You will use Sencha Command to optimize your code for a production environment.

You also need a web server running on your development computer, and a browser to test the application. Google Chrome is a good choice for this purpose.

Testing the application in Chrome will allow you to take advantage of Chrome's Developer Tools to debug your code. You can access these tools from Chrome's settings:

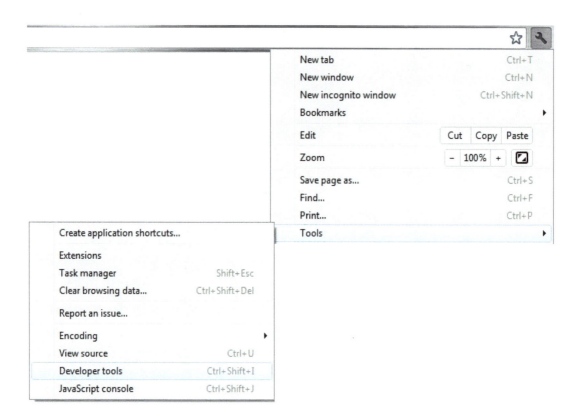

Throughout the book, you will notice that I have adorned the application screenshots with a mobile phone skin:

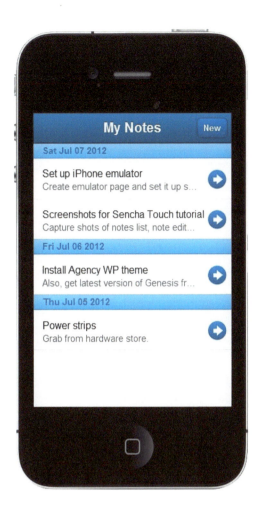

Although the results that you will see in Chrome will not have this skin, the application's look in the browser will be very close to its look on a mobile device.

The application's directories and files

A Sencha Touch application consists of a number of HTML, JavaScript, CSS, images and data files. These files can be static or generated dynamically.

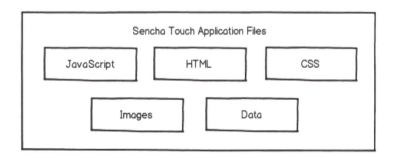

You will organize the source code in a directories tree similar to this:

You will place your files under the *NotesApp* directory, with the application's setup code in the NotesApp/app.js file.

The *app* directory will contain the *controller*, *model*, *profile*, *store*, and *view* directories. Any controllers, models, profiles, stores and views used in the application will reside in these directories.

The index.html file will launch the app. In it, you will include the Sencha Touch Framework files and the application's main JavaScript file:

- sencha-touch.css
- sencha-touch-debug.js
- app.js

This is the source for the index.html file:

```html
<!DOCTYPE html>
<html>
<head>
    <title>My Notes</title>
    <link href="../../lib/st2.4.0/resources/css/sencha-touch.css"
rel="stylesheet" type="text/css" />
    <script src="../../lib/st2.4.0/sencha-touch-debug.js"
type="text/javascript"></script>
    <script src="app.js" type="text/javascript"></script>
</head>
```

```
<body>

</body>
</html>
```

Notice that you will keeping the Framework's files in the Lib/ST2.4.0 directory:

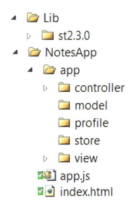

You are also using the sencha-touch-debug.js build of the Framework, which Sencha recommends to develop and debug applications locally.

When you are ready to run the application in production, you can switch to the sencha-touch.js file, which you can use with a custom build that includes only the Framework classes used by the application. This will reduce the number of requests to the server and the download time, allowing the application to launch faster.

Creating the Application instance

Our first step in the app.js file will consist of creating an instance of the Sencha Touch *Ext.app.Application* class. This class defines the set of models, controllers, profiles, stores and views that an application consists of.

You are going to define an *Application* instance using the *Ext.application* method:

```
Ext.application({
    name: 'NotesApp',

    launch: function () {
```

```
        console.log('App launch');
    }
});
```

Thanks to the *application* method you do not need to use *Ext.create*, the method normally used to create class instances in Sencha Touch, to create an *Application* instance.

The *application* method instantiates the *Ext.app.Application* class, automatically loading the class if it is not present on the page, and binding to the *Ext.onReady* method before creating the instance itself. It also triggers the load of the models, views, controllers, stores and profiles the application depends on, if they were defined using the *models, views, controllers, stores* and *profiles* config objects.

The *launch* method is invoked as soon as the app loads its dependencies and instantiates its controllers.

If you navigate to the index.html page using Google Chrome and enable Chrome's JavaScript console, you should see the following message:

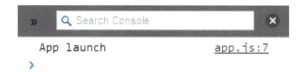

Where are we?

In this chapter we defined the application that you will create in this book, along with its features and views.

You also learned what a Sencha Touch application is, which directory structure is recommended for a Sencha Touch application, and how the *Application* class works.

Now you are ready to start building the application's user interface. Let's see how it is done.

Chapter 2: Rendering Cached Notes

What you will learn in this chapter

In this chapter you are going to start building the NotesList view. This view is an example of a list-based user interface, one of the most popular user interface styles in mobile applications.

In the process of building the NotesList view, you will learn the following topics:

- How to create a list-based user interface using Sencha Touch's List component.
- How to create a Sencha Touch model, and how to define model validations.
- How to create a data store in Sencha Touch, and how a store and its model work together.
- How to bind a Sencha Touch List to a data store.
- How to modify the look of the items of a Sencha Touch List.
- How to use the Sencha Touch TitleBar component.

Defining a view in Sencha Touch

The main view of the application will render a list of notes. To build this view, you will use an instance of the *Container* class, which will host a *Toolbar* and a *List* component:

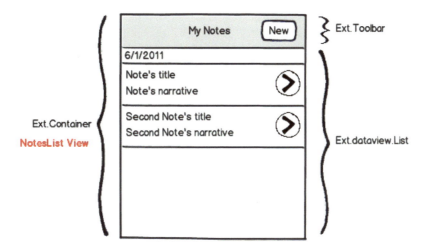

As a first step, you will create the NotesList.js file in the *view* directory:

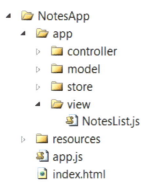

You will then define the NotesList class in the NotesList.js file:

```
Ext.define('NotesApp.view.NotesList', {
    extend: 'Ext.Container',
    requires:['Ext.TitleBar'],
    alias: 'widget.noteslistview',
    config: {
        layout: {
            type: 'fit'
        },
        items: [{
            xtype: 'titlebar',
            title: 'My Notes',
            docked: 'top',
            items: [
                {
                    xtype: 'button',
                    text: 'New',
```

```
                ui: 'action',
                itemId: 'newButton',
                align: 'right'
            }
        ]
    }]
    }
});
```

You are using *Ext.define* and the *extend* config to define an extension to the *Ext.Container* class.

As you will use a *TitleBar* instance for the view's toolbar, you need to add the *requires* config. This guarantees that the *Ext.Loader* will download the source of the *TitleBar* component.

The *Ext.Loader* singleton is very helpful during application development, as it allows applications to download their dependencies on the fly.

In the *TitleBar* configuration, the *docked* config allows you to dock the *TitleBar* to the top region of the view. The *TitleBar* will in turn contain one *Button*, the New button, which will allow users to activate the NoteEditor view when they need to create a new note. Additionally, you use the *align* config to place the New button on the right end of the *TitleBar*.

Setting the value of the *ui* config to *action* gives the New button a distinctive look, indicating that it represents the default button on the view.

The *alias* config of the NotesList class will allow you to refer to the class by its *xtype*, which is simply a shortcut for its full name, as you will see next.

Adding the view to the application

With the *NotesList* class defined, it is time to make the *Application* aware of it. Back in the app.js file, you are going to add the *views* config to the *application* method:

```
Ext.application({
    name: 'NotesApp',

    views: ['NotesList'],

    launch: function () {

        var notesListView = {
            xtype: 'noteslistview'
        };

        Ext.Viewport.add([notesListView]);

    }
});
```

You inform the *Application* that it has a dependency on the NoteList view by using the *views* config:

```
views: ['NotesList'],
```

By default, the *Application* class expects its models, views, controllers, stores and profiles to exist in the app/model, app/view, app/controller, app/store, and app/profile directories. If you follow this convention, you can define models, views, controllers, stores and profiles using the last part of their names, as you do here. If you use a different directory structure, you can still refer to the application's components using their fully qualified names.

After adding the NotesList view to the *views* config, you create an instance of this view in the app's *launch* method. Finally, you add the view to the app's viewport:

```
var notesListView = {
    xtype: 'noteslistview'
};

Ext.Viewport.add([notesListView]);
```

It is time to check out how the NotesList view looks. Opening the index.html file in your favorite WebKit-powered browser should produce something similar to the screenshot below:

Configuring the notes list

Our next step in the NotesList view is to add the component that will render the list of cached notes. Back in the NotesList.js file, you will add an *Ext.dataview.List* instance to the *items* config like so:

```
Ext.define('NotesApp.view.NotesList', {
    extend: 'Ext.Container',
    requires:['Ext.TitleBar','Ext.dataview.List'],
    alias: 'widget.noteslistview',
```

```
config: {
    layout: {
        type: 'fit'
    },
    items: [{
        xtype: 'titlebar',
        title: 'My Notes',
        docked: 'top',
        items: [
            {
                xtype: 'button',
                text: 'New',
                ui: 'action',
                itemId: 'newButton',
                align: 'right'
            }
        ]
    },{
        xtype: 'list',
        store:[],
        itemId: 'notesList',
        itemCls: 'list-item-custom',
        loadingText: 'Loading Notes...',
        emptyText: '<div>No notes found.</div>',
        onItemDisclosure: true,
        itemTpl: '<div>{title}</div><div>{narrative}</div>'
    }]
    }
});
```

Notice that you added the *Ext.dataview.List* entry to the *requires* config of the view.

Now, let's look at the list's definition in detail:

```
{
    xtype: 'list',
    store:[],
    itemId: 'notesList',
    itemCls: 'list-item-custom',
    loadingText: 'Loading Notes...',
    emptyText: '<div>No notes found.</div>',
    onItemDisclosure: true,
    itemTpl: '<div>{title}</div><div>{narrative}</div>'
```

```
}
```

As you did with the *TitleBar* instance, you are using the *xtype* config to lazy-instantiate the list. For now, the list's store is an empty array. In the next section of this chapter you will create the *Store* component that will feed the list.

The itemCls config will allow you to use a css class to customize the look of the list items.

The *emptyText* and *itemTpl* configs control how the "empty list" message and the list's items will render.

Setting the *onItemDisclosure* config to *true* causes the list to render a *disclose* icon next to each list item:

Later in the book you will use the *disclose* icon as well as the *itemId* config to define a handler method for the list's *disclose* event. This is how you will load an existing note into the NoteEditor view.

A data model for notes

For the NotesList view to work, you need to define a Sencha Touch model that will represent a note. Let's create the Note.js file in the app/model directory:

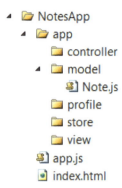

NotesApp
  app
    controller
    model
      Note.js
    profile
    store
    view
  app.js
  index.html

Now you can create the model's definition as follows:

```
Ext.define('NotesApp.model.Note', {
    extend: 'Ext.data.Model',
    config: {
        idProperty: 'id',
        fields: [
            { name: 'id', type: 'int' },
            { name: 'dateCreated', type: 'date', dateFormat: 'c' },
            { name: 'title', type: 'string' },
            { name: 'narrative', type: 'string' }
        ],
        validations: [
            { type: 'presence', field: 'id' },
            { type: 'presence', field: 'dateCreated' },
            { type: 'presence', field: 'title', message: 'Please enter
a title for this note.' }
        ]
    }
});
```

A note will have four fields: *id*, *dateCreated*, *title* and *narrative*. You will use the *idProperty* config to establish that the *id* field is actually the field that Sencha Touch will use to identify a note.

This seems trivial in this case because you have total control over the names of the fields of the model. However, you might encounter cases where the model's fields are tightly coupled to column names in an existing database, and the name of the column that uniquely identifies a record is not *id*. This is why the *idProperty* config is important.

Defining model validations

The *id*, *dateCreated* and *title* fields in the Note model are mandatory. You will define this requirement using the *validations* config:

```
validations: [
    { type: 'presence', field: 'id' },
    { type: 'presence', field: 'dateCreated' },
    { type: 'presence', field: 'title', message: 'Please enter a title
for this note.' }
]
```

For the *title* field, you are taking advantage of the *message* config to define the message the user will see when she tries to save a note without typing in its title.

Before moving on to create the data store for the NotesList view, you need to add the model to the *models* config of the application. Among other things, this will allow the *Ext.Loader* to download the model's file, app/model/Note.js.

You will declare the Note model in the app.js file:

```
Ext.application({
    name: 'NotesApp',

    views: ['NotesList'],
    models: ['Note'],

    launch: function () {

        var notesListView = {
            xtype: 'noteslistview'
        };

        Ext.Viewport.add([notesListView]);

    }
```

```
});
```

The Notes store

Let's now focus on creating the Sencha Touch store that will feed the NotesList view. You will define the Notes store goes in a new file, Notes.js, which you will pplace in the app/store directory:

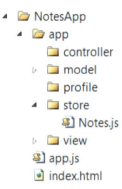

This is the definition of the store:

```
Ext.define('NotesApp.store.Notes', {
    extend: 'Ext.data.Store',
    config: {
        model: 'NotesApp.model.Note',
        data: [
            { title: 'Note 1', narrative: 'narrative 1' },
            { title: 'Note 2', narrative: 'narrative 2' }
        ],
        autoLoad: true,
        sorters: [{ property: 'dateCreated', direction: 'DESC'}]
    }
});
```

For now, the Notes store will simply contain a few hard-coded records, defined through the *data* config. You will use the *model* config to specify that this store will contain instances of the Note model, and the *sorters* config to render the notes sorted by creation date. Sorters usually require the *property* to sort by and the *direction* of the sort. They can also accept custom sort methods.

Now you need to jump back to the app.js file, and declare the Notes store as part of the Application's definition. You will do this through the app's *stores* config:

```
Ext.application({
    name: 'NotesApp',

    views: ['NotesList'],
    models: ['Note'],
    stores: ['Notes'],

    launch: function () {

        var notesListView = {
            xtype: 'noteslistview'
        };

        Ext.Viewport.add([notesListView]);

    }
});
```

As with the *views* and *models* configs, declaring the Notes store with the *stores* config allows the *Ext.Loader* to download its file and instantiate the store for us.

Binding the notes list to the store

After adding the store to the application, return to the NotesList.js file and add the store to the List declaration in the NotesList class:

```
Ext.define('NotesApp.view.NotesList', {
    extend: 'Ext.Container',
    requires:['Ext.TitleBar','Ext.dataview.List'],
    alias: 'widget.noteslistview',

    config: {
        layout: {
            type: 'fit'
        },
        items: [{
            xtype: 'titlebar',
            title: 'My Notes',
```

```
            docked: 'top',
            items: [
                {
                    xtype: 'button',
                    text: 'New',
                    ui: 'action',
                    itemId: 'newButton',
                    align: 'right'
                }
            ]
        }, {
            xtype: 'list',
            store: 'Notes',       // Store
            itemId: 'notesList',
            itemCls: 'list-item-custom',
            loadingText: 'Loading Notes...',
            emptyText: '<div>No notes found.</div>',
            onItemDisclosure: true,
            itemTpl: '<div>{title}</div><div>{narrative}</div>'
        }]
    }
});
```

The *store* config accepts an *Ext.data.Store* instance, a configuration object that the Framework can use to create a store, or the name of an existing store.

You will use the third approach in the NotesList class:

```
{
    xtype: 'list',
    store: 'Notes',       // Store
    itemId: 'notesList',
    itemCls: 'list-item-custom',
    loadingText: 'Loading Notes...',
    emptyText: '<div>No notes found.</div>',
    onItemDisclosure: true,
    itemTpl: '<div>{title}</div><div>{narrative}</div>'
}]
```

Using a store name is possible because the *Ext.dataview.List* component has the ability to invoke the *Ext.data.StoreManager.lookup* method, which can look up a store by name.

Great! At this point you should be able to see the hard-coded notes rendered on the screen. If you open the index.html file with your favorite WebKit browser, you should see something like this:

Styling list items

How about applying some styling to the list items in order to give the list a more polished look? Let's create the resources/css directory under the app's root, and in it, the app.css file:

```
   ⊿ 📂 NotesApp
      ▷ 📁 app
      ⊿ 📁 resources
         ⊿ 📁 css
               🅰 app.css
      📳 app.js
      📄 index.html
```

Add the following classes in the app.css file:

```css
/* Center the disclosure button vertically */
.x-list .x-list-item.list-item-custom .x-list-disclosure {
    margin-top:13px;
}
.list-item-title
{
    height:1em;
    width:100%;
    white-space: nowrap;
    overflow: hidden;
    text-overflow: ellipsis;
    padding-right:25px;
    margin-bottom:5px;
}
.list-item-narrative
{
    height:1em;
    width:95%;
    color:#666666;
    white-space: nowrap;
    overflow: hidden;
    text-overflow: ellipsis;
    padding-right:25px;
    font-size:80%;
}

.x-item-selected .list-item-title
{
    color:#ffffff;
}
```

```
.x-item-selected .list-item-narrative
{
    color:#ffffff;
}
.notes-list-empty-text
{
    padding:10px;
}
```

The *list-item-custom* class, assigned to the list's *itemCls* config, shifts the disclosure button vertically. The *list-item-title* and *list-item-narrative* classes control the styles of each row. Here you are simply setting the font color of each list item to white when the item is selected. This will give you white text over the blue background of Sencha Touch's default theme.

Now you need to include app.css in the index.html file:

```
<!DOCTYPE html>
<html>
<head>
    <title>My Notes</title>
    <link href="../../lib/st2.4.0/resources/css/sencha-touch.css"
rel="stylesheet" type="text/css" />
    <link href="resources/css/app.css" rel="stylesheet"
type="text/css" />
    <script src="../../lib/st2.4.0/sencha-touch-debug.js"
type="text/javascript"></script>
    <script src="app.js" type="text/javascript"></script>
</head>
<body>

</body>
</html>
```

Then, in the NotesList view definition, modify the List's *emptyText* and *itemTpl* configs as follows:

```
{
    xtype: 'list',
    store: 'Notes',
```

```
    itemId: 'notesList', ,
    itemCls: 'list-item-custom',
    loadingText: 'Loading Notes...',
    emptyText: '<div class="notes-list-empty-text">No notes
found.</div>',
    onItemDisclosure: true,
    itemTpl: '<div class="list-item-title">{title}</div><div
class="list-item-narrative">{narrative}</div>'
}
```

Adding the *notes-list-empty-text*, *list-item-title* and *list-item-narrative* classes to
the configs will result in a more attractive list:

Where are we?

While building the NotesList view, you learned how to create a Sencha Touch List component, its data store, model and model validations. You also learned a simple approach to style list items.

The Notes application now has the ability to render the notes cached in a store. Although these notes are currently hard-coded, later you will learn how to take advantage of the HTML5's localStorage API to persist notes across browser sessions.

You next steps will take you to a very important domain in Sencha Touch - working with controllers.

Chapter 3: Creating the Controller

What you will learn in this chapter

You are going to start this chapter by creating custom events based on the actions the users of the application will take on the NotesList view. Then, you will create the controller instance that will listen to these events and perform the desired application logic.

Here are the topics that you will learn in this chapter:

- How to listen to component events within a Sencha Touch view.
- How to convert component events into view events, and how to publish these view events.
- How to instantiate a Sencha Touch controller, and how a controller works.

Publishing an event when a toolbar button is tapped

An important feature that you need to add to the NotesList view is the ability to activate the NoteEditor view when a user wants to add, edit or delete a note.

When a user wants to create a new note, she will tap the New button. In the view, you are going to use the *listeners* config to define a *tap* listener for this button.

The *listeners* config goes in the view/NotesList.js file, immediately after the *items* array:

```
items: [
    // Items omitted for brevity...
],
listeners: [{
    delegate: '#newButton',
    event: 'tap',
    fn: 'onNewButtonTap'
```

```
}]
```

In the listener, the *delegate* config informs the view that you want to bind the listener to the component that matches the *#newButton* selector. The *fn* config is a pointer to the method that will handle the *tap* event.

You are going to define the *tap* handler method right after the view's *config* object:

```
config: {
    // config contents omitted for brevity...
},
onNewButtonTap: function () {
    console.log('newNoteCommand');
    this.fireEvent('newNoteCommand', this);
}
```

The *onNewButtonTap* method transforms the *tap* event on the button into an event that is more descriptive of the application's business logic. You will call this custom event *newNoteCommand*.

The controller class, which you will define in a few minutes, will use this event to create a new note and load it into the NoteEditor view.

Advantages of creating custom events in a view

Transforming component-specific events into view events is an approach that you might want to use in many scenarios, because it has the following benefits:

- It produces cleaner view interfaces, as the views fire events that are more in line with the business logic of the application. For example, think about a view firing a *tap* event versus firing a *createFavorite* event.

- It produces views and controllers that are easier to modify and maintain, as a controller does not need intimate knowledge of the view's inner workings. For example, think about a view where a *tap* on a toolbar button fires a *createFavorite* event, which later needs to be changed so the *createFavorite* event is fired instead by a *tap* on a list item. In such a case, the controller would not need modifications. It would always listen to the view's *createFavorite* event, and not to *tap* events of any of the view's components.

If you navigate to the index.html page using Google Chrome, enable Chrome's JavaScript console, and tap the New button on the NotesList view, you should see a log entry for the *newNoteCommand* event:

```
newNoteCommand          NotesList.js:39
>
```

Publishing an event when a list item is tapped

When a user needs to edit a note, she will tap the disclosure button for the given note. This is how the disclosure buttons will look in the finished application:

In order to trigger the activation of the NoteEditor view when the user taps a note's disclosure button, you need to define a *disclose* listener for the List:

```
listeners: [{
    delegate: '#newButton',
    event: 'tap',
    fn: 'onNewButtonTap'
}, {
    delegate: '#notesList',
    event: 'disclose',
    fn: 'onNotesListDisclose'
}]
```

This listener is similar to the one you created for the New button. The *delegate* points to the List's *itemId*, and *fn* is the *onNotesListDisclose* method, which you are going to create immediately after *onNewButtonTap*:

```
onNewButtonTap: function () {
    console.log('newNoteCommand');
    this.fireEvent('newNoteCommand', this);
},
onNotesListDisclose: function (list, record, target, index, evt,
options) {
    console.log('editNoteCommand');
    this.fireEvent('editNoteCommand', this, record);
}
```

You are transforming the component-specific *disclose* event into a custom view event called *editNoteCommand*. You are broadcasting this event from the view. The controller will use it to load the selected note into the Note Editor.

Notice that one of the arguments of the *editNoteCommand* event is the actual *record* containing the selected note's data.

A quick check on Chrome's JavaScript console should show the *editNoteCommand* message when you tap the disclosure button of any list item:

```
editNoteCommand            NotesList.js:47
>
```

Defining and instantiating a controller

The role of a controller consists of translating the user's input, captured by the views, into changes to the application's state and behavior. The first functions that you need the application's controller to perform are to capture the events fired from the NotesList view, and load either a new or the selected note into the NoteEditor view.

Let's define a very simple controller class. You will place this class in the Notes.js file, which you will save to the app/controller directory:

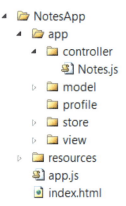

This is the controller's definition:

```
Ext.define('NotesApp.controller.Notes', {

    extend: 'Ext.app.Controller',

    // Base class methods.
    launch: function () {
        this.callParent(arguments);
        console.log('launch');
    },
    init: function () {
        this.callParent(arguments);
        console.log('init');
    }
});
```

Sencha Touch controllers contain a couple of methods, *init* and *launch*, that run at different moments during the Application's startup process.

Before the Application's *launch* method runs, Sencha Touch invokes the controller's *init* method. After the Application's *launch* method, the Framework invokes the controller's *launch* method:

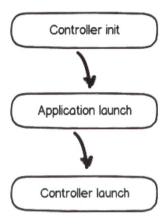

It is important that you know the order in which these methods run, as they allow you to perform initialization code at different times while an application is starting up.

For now, your *launch* and *init* methods will simply call the *init* and *launch* methods of the parent class. This is why you use the *callParent* function:

```
launch: function () {
    this.callParent(arguments);
    console.log('launch');
},
init: function () {
    this.callParent(arguments);
    console.log('init');
}
```

You will make the Application aware of the Notes controller class by adding this controller to the app's *controllers* config:

```
Ext.application({
    name: 'NotesApp',

    models: ['Note'],
    views: ['NotesList'],
    controllers: ['Notes'],
    stores: ['Notes'],

    launch: function () {
```

```
        var notesListView = {
            xtype: 'noteslistview'
        };

        Ext.Viewport.add([notesListView]);

    }
});
```

As you already know, having the Notes controller class listed in the *controllers*
config will cause the Application to automatically instantiate and hold a reference
to this controller.

How controllers listen to view events

The first feature you will add to the Notes controller is the ability to handle the
newNoteCommand event fired from the NotesList view.

You can accomplish this by first adding the *refs* and *control* objects to the
controller's *config*:

```
Ext.define('NotesApp.controller.Notes', {

    extend: 'Ext.app.Controller',

    config: {
        refs: {
            // We're going to look up our views by xtype.
            notesListView: 'noteslistview'
        },
        control: {
            notesListView: {
                // The commands fired by the notes list.
                newNoteCommand: 'onNewNoteCommand'
            }
        }
    },

    // Base class methods.
```

```
launch: function () {
    this.callParent(arguments);
    console.log('launch');
},
init: function () {
    this.callParent(arguments);
    console.log('init');
}
});
```

The *refs* and *control* objects are at the heart of the mechanism by which a controller acquires references to the Application's views and other components, and defines event handlers for them.

Refs give the controller the ability to find components in the app. They use Sencha Touch's *ComponentQuery* class, which retrieves components using a CSS selector-like syntax.

In the Notes controller, the *notesListView* ref creates a reference to the Component whose alias is *noteslistview*, which is the NotesList view.

```
refs: {
    // We're going to look up our views by xtype.
    notesListView: 'noteslistview'
},
```

Based on this *ref*, the framework generates a hidden getter method that you can use to work with the NotesList view reference if you need to.

Sencha Touch names ref-derived getter methods following a simple format that consists of the word *get* and the capitalized name of the ref in question. In this case, the name of the method will be *getNotesListView*.

Refs also give you the ability to instantiate the components they reference if such instances do not already exist. This feature is very useful in large applications where you cannot afford or do not need to instantiate all the application's components upon application launch.

The *control* config allows you to define event handlers for any of the Application's Components. You can use *refs* or *ComponentQuery* selectors to define event handlers within *control*. In the Notes controller, the *notesListView ref* defines a handler for the *newNoteCommand* event:

```
control: {
    notesListView: {
        // The commands fired by the notes list.
        newNoteCommand: 'onNewNoteCommand'
    }
}
```

Youe also need to define the handler method, which you will do immediately after the controller's *config*:

```
onNewNoteCommand: function () {

    console.log('onNewNoteCommand');

},
```

The *onNewNoteCommand* method is simply writing a message to the browser's JavaScript console. This is where you will later add the code that opens the Note Editor.

Let's take a moment to check the application on Google Chrome. In particular, what happens when you tap the New button in the NotesList view. If a tap occurs, Chrome's JavaScript console should display the message you placed in the *onNewNoteCommand* method:

```
init                              Notes.js:32
launch                            Notes.js:28
newNoteCommand               NotesList.js:43
onNewNoteCommand                  Notes.js:21
    >
```

One important takeaway from this book is that when you need your controller to handle a particular view event, you can follow these steps:

1. Create a *ref* for the component in the controller's *refs* config.

2. Create an entry for the *ref* in the controller's *control* config.

3. Use the entry in the *control* config to specify the handler for the events in which you are interested.

The other event of the NotesList view that you need to handle in the controller is *editNoteCommand*. The view fires this event when a user taps the *disclosure* button of any items of the NotesList view:

You will handle the *editNoteCommand* event by first mapping the event to a handler method in the controller's *control* config:

```
control: {
    notesListView: {
        // The commands fired by the notes list.
        newNoteCommand: 'onNewNoteCommand',
        editNoteCommand: 'onEditNoteCommand'
    }
}
```

Then, define the *onEditNoteCommand* method like so:

```
onEditNoteCommand: function (list, record) {
```

```
    console.log('onEditNoteCommand');
},
```

Notice how the *list* and *record* arguments correspond to those of the NotesList view's *editNoteCommand* event.

A quick check with Google Chrome should show that tapping a *disclosure* button on any list item creates a log entry with the *onEditNoteCommand* message in the JavaScript console:

```
init                              Notes.js:38
launch                            Notes.js:34
editNoteCommand                   NotesList.js:47
onEditNoteCommand                 Notes.js:27
  >
```

Where are we?

In this chapter you connected the NotesList view to the application's sole controller. You learned how to create event listeners for different components in a Sencha Touch view, and how to create and publish custom events.

You spent time learning how to instantiate a Sencha Touch controller, and how to use the controller configs that allow it to listen to view events.

At this point, you have a functioning NotesList view and a controller with event handlers bound to the view's events.

In the next chapter you will start building the user interface that will let users edit, save and delete notes.

Chapter 4: Loading Notes into the Editor

What you will learn in this chapter

In this chapter you are going to switch gears and start learning how to use Sencha Touch form components to capture user input. The goal is to build the NoteEditor view.

While building the NoteEditor view, you will learn the following topics:

- How to create a Sencha Touch form panel.
- How to create a new note and load it into the NoteEditor view.
- How to load an existing note into the NoteEditor view.
- How to publish events from within the NoteEditor view.

Creating a form in Sencha Touch

The NoteEditor view will allow users to create, edit and delete notes. This is how the finished view will look:

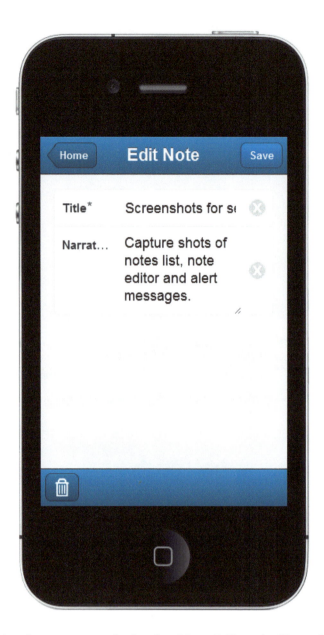

You will place the view's source code in the NoteEditor.js file, which you will create in the app/view directory:

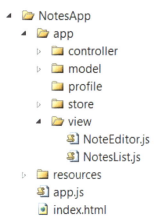

In the NoteEditor.js file, you will define an empty NoteEditor class:

```
Ext.define('NotesApp.view.NoteEditor', {
    extend: 'Ext.form.Panel',
    alias: 'widget.noteeditorview',
    config: {
        scrollable: 'vertical'
    }
});
```

The NoteEditor class is an extension of the *Ext.form.Panel* class. The *scrollable* config allows the contents of the *Panel* to scroll vertically. This prevents the mobile device's browser from cropping the form when the form's height is greater than the screen height of the device, which is likely to happen if someone uses the app in landscape mode.

As you did with the NotesList class, you are going to use the *config* object to define the NoteEditor's components:

```
Ext.define('NotesApp.view.NoteEditor', {
    extend: 'Ext.form.Panel',
    requires: ['Ext.Toolbar','Ext.form.FieldSet', 'Ext.form.Text',
'Ext.field.TextArea','Ext.MessageBox'],
    alias: 'widget.noteeditorview',
    config: {
        scrollable: 'vertical',
        items: [
            {
```

```
    xtype: 'titlebar',
    docked: 'top',
    title: 'Edit Note',
    items: [
        {
            xtype: 'button',
            ui: 'back',
            text: 'Home',
            itemId: 'backButton',
            align: 'left'
        },
        {
            xtype: 'button',
            ui: 'action',
            text: 'Save',
            itemId: 'saveButton',
            align: 'right'
        }
    ]
},
{
    xtype: 'toolbar',
    docked: 'bottom',
    items: [
        {
            xtype: 'button',
            iconCls: 'trash',
            iconMask: true,
            itemId: 'deleteButton'
        }
    ]
},
{ xtype: 'fieldset',
    items: [
        {
            xtype: 'textfield',
            name: 'title',
            label: 'Title',
            required: true
        },
        {
            xtype: 'textareafield',
            name: 'narrative',
            label: 'Narrative'
        }
```

```
              ]
          }
      ]
   }
});
```

In the *config* object, you first define the *TitleBar*, along with its two buttons, the Home button and the Save button. Then you define the bottom *Toolbar* and the Delete button. Notice that docking a *Toolbar* to the bottom of a container is achieved with the *docked='bottom'* config.

Next, you add the fields used to edit the note's title and narrative. They are instances of the *Ext.form.Text* and *Ext.form.TextArea* classes. By placing them inside a *FieldSet* component, you give the form a more polished look.

The *requires* config forces the *Ext.Loader* to download the code for the *FieldSet*, *TextField*, *TextAreaField* and *MessageBox* components:

```
Ext.define(requires, {
    extend: 'Ext.form.Panel',
    requires: ['Ext.Toolbar','Ext.form.FieldSet', 'Ext.form.Text',
'Ext.field.TextArea','Ext.MessageBox'],
    alias: 'widget.noteeditor',
    config: {
        scrollable: 'vertical'
    },

    // Rest of the class omitted for brevity.

});
```

Loading a new note

Before continuing the implementation of the NoteEditor view, you are going to work on the code that will render the editor when a user taps the New button in the NotesList view.

Earlier in the book, you created the *tap* handler for the New button, which fires the *newNoteCommand* event. You also added the *onNewNoteCommand* listener to the Notes controller. You will use this method to activate the NoteEditor view.

Let's jump to the controller's file, controller/Notes.js. In order to activate the NoteEditor view, you first need to create a reference for it. You will use the *noteEditorView ref* for this purpose:

```
Ext.define('NotesApp.controller.Notes', {

    extend: 'Ext.app.Controller',

    config: {
        refs: {
            // We're going to look up our views by xtype.
            notesListView: 'noteslistview',
            noteEditorView: 'noteeditorview'
        }
    }

    // Rest of controller omitted for brevity.
});
```

This *ref* automatically creates a hidden *getNoteEditorView* method in the controller, which you can use to refer to the NoteEditor instance.

Next, you need to implement the *onNewNoteCommand* method:

```
onNewNoteCommand: function () {

    console.log('onNewNoteCommand');

    var now = new Date();
    var noteId = (now.getTime()).toString() + (this.getRandomInt(0,
100)).toString();

    var newNote = Ext.create('NotesApp.model.Note', {
        id: noteId,
        dateCreated: now,
        title: '',
```

```
        narrative: ''
    });

    this.activateNoteEditor(newNote);

},
```

In *onNewNoteCommand*, you create a new note and pass it to the *activateNoteEditor* method.

The *getRamdomInt* method will generate an integer that you will use to create a unique *id* for each new note. Let's add it to the Note controller:

```
getRandomInt: function (min, max) {
    return Math.floor(Math.random() * (max - min + 1)) + min;
},
```

After creating the new note, the *activateNoteEditor* method will first load the note into the NoteEditor view, and then make the view active:

```
activateNoteEditor: function (record) {

    var noteEditorView = this.getNoteEditorView();
    noteEditorView.setRecord(record);
    Ext.Viewport.animateActiveItem(noteEditorView,
this.slideLeftTransition);
},
```

Here you are taking advantage of the *Ext.form.Panel*'s *setRecord* method, which loads the values of a model instance into a form's fields, as long as the field names match those of the model's fields.

The activateNoteEditor method also uses the *slideLeftTransition* variable, which you need to define at the top of the controller like so:

```
slideLeftTransition: { type: 'slide', direction: 'left' }
```

When you call *Ext.Viewport.animateActiveItem*, the transition will bring the NoteEditor into view with a slide motion from the right to the left.

This is all the controller needs to do in order to activate the NoteEditor view when a user taps the New button.

However, you need to make the application aware of the *NoteEditor* class. In the app.js file, you will add the new view to the *views* config:

```
views: ['NotesList', 'NoteEditor'],
```

You are also going to define an instance of the NoteEditor view and add it to the *Viewport*:

```
Ext.application({
    name: 'NotesApp',

    models: ['Note'],
    stores: ['Notes'],
    controllers: ['Notes'],
    views: ['NotesList', 'NoteEditor'],

    launch: function () {

        var notesListView = {
            xtype: 'noteslistview'
        };
        var noteEditorView = {
            xtype: 'noteeditorview'
        };

        Ext.Viewport.add([notesListView, noteEditorView]);


    }
});
```

Ready to check it out? After opening the index.html file in your favorite WebKit browser, a tap on the New button of the NotesList view should render the NoteEditor view:

Editing an existing note

When a user needs to edit an existing note, she will tap the note's *disclosure* button on the NotesList view:

When this happens, the NotesList view fires the *editNoteCommand* event, which you mapped to the *onEditNoteCommand* method in the controller:

```
control: {
    notesListView: {
        // The commands fired by the notes list.
        newNoteCommand: 'onNewNoteCommand',
        editNoteCommand: 'onEditNoteCommand'
    }
}
```

Let's implement the *onEditNoteCommand* method like so:

```
onEditNoteCommand: function (list, record) {

    console.log('onEditNoteCommand');

    this.activateNoteEditor(record);
},
```

This is a very simple implementation where you call the controller's *activateNoteEditor* method, passing the *record* argument, which contains the selected note's data.

Now you are going to open the index.html file with your favorite WebKit browser. After the NotesList view renders, a tap on a note's disclosure button should load the note into the NoteEditor view:

Publishing events from the Note Editor view

You need to create listeners for three events in the NoteEditor view. The first

listener is going to allow a user to save her note when she taps the Save button. In

the view/NoteEditor.js file, immediately after the *items* array, declare this listener

as follows:

```
items:[
     // items omitted for brevity...
],
```

```
listeners: [
    {
        delegate: '#saveButton',
        event: 'tap',
        fn: 'onSaveButtonTap'
    }
]
```

The *delegate* config of the listener is the value of the *itemId* config of the button.
The *fn* config is a pointer to the method that will handle the *tap* event. You will
define this method right after the view's *config* object:

```
config:{
    // configs omitted for brevity...
},
onSaveButtonTap: function () {
    console.log('saveNoteCommand');
    this.fireEvent('saveNoteCommand', this);
}
```

The *onSaveButtonTap* method captures a *tap* event on the button, and transforms it
into an event that is more specific and descriptive of the application's business
logic. You will call this event *saveNoteCommand*. The controller will use this event
to save the edited note and activate the NotesList view.

Did you notice that these steps are similar to those you followed when you
published the NotesList view's events?

The next listener will take care of *tap* events on the Delete button. You will add this
listener to the view's *listeners* config:

```
listeners: [
    {
        delegate: '#saveButton',
        event: 'tap',
        fn: 'onSaveButtonTap'
    },
    {
```

```
        delegate: '#deleteButton',
        event: 'tap',
        fn: 'onDeleteButtonTap'
    }
]
```

The *delegate* config of this listener is the value of the *itemId* config of the Delete
button. The *fn* config points to the *onDeleteButtonTap* method, which you will
define like so:

```
onDeleteButtonTap: function () {
    console.log('deleteNoteCommand');
    this.fireEvent('deleteNoteCommand', this);
}
```

The *onDeleteButtonTap* method transforms the *tap* event of the button into the
view's *deleteNoteCommand* event. The controller will use this event to delete the
note loaded into the view.

Last, but not least, is the handler for the Back button's *tap* event:

```
listeners: [
    {
        delegate: '#saveButton',
        event: 'tap',
        fn: 'onSaveButtonTap'
    },
    {
        delegate: '#deleteButton',
        event: 'tap',
        fn: 'onDeleteButtonTap'
    },
    {

        delegate: '#backButton',
        event: 'tap',
        fn: 'onBackButtonTap'
    }
]
```

This listener binds the button's *tap* event to the *onBackButtonTap* method. You will define *onBackButtonTap* as follows:

```
onBackButtonTap: function () {
    console.log('backToHomeCommand');
    this.fireEvent('backToHomeCommand', this);
}
```

You use this method to publish the *backToHomeCommand* event when a user taps the Back button.

If you check the app with Google Chrome, you should be able to see the three messages you are logging in the JavaScript console:

```
init
launch
newNoteCommand
onNewNoteCommand
saveNoteCommand
deleteNoteCommand
backToHomeCommand
>
```

Where are we?

In this chapter you created the NoteEditor view, which consists of a Sencha Touch Form Panel and a couple of toolbars. You learned how to define new notes, and how to load both new and existing notes into the NoteEditor view.

After setting up the components of the NoteEditor view, you created the view events that, captured by the controller, will give the application the ability to save and delete notes.

Now it is time now to work on the ability to save notes.

Chapter 5: Saving Notes

What you will learn in this chapter

The ability to save data on the device is an essential feature of any mobile application. In this chapter you will to add this feature to you application.

These are the specific topics you will learn in this chapter:

- How Sencha Touch allows you to leverage the localStorage API to save data on the device running the application.
- How to handle validation errors in a Sencha Touch model.
- How to add and edit records in a Sencha Touch store.

Using a localStorage proxy in Sencha Touch

Before you shift your attention to the controller, which needs to capture and handle the events you created in the NoteEditor view, you will to stop using hard-coded notes as the data for the Notes store.

Up to this point, you have been using the *data* config to define a few hard-coded records in the store:

```
Ext.define('NotesApp.store.Notes', {
    extend: 'Ext.data.Store',
    config: {
        model: 'NotesApp.model.Note',
        data: [
            { title: 'Note 1', narrative: 'narrative 1' },
            { title: 'Note 2', narrative: 'narrative 2' }
        ],
        autoLoad: true,
        sorters: [{ property: 'dateCreated', direction: 'DESC'}]
    }
});
```

As you intend to cache notes on the device that runs the app, you are going to discontinue the *data* config in the Notes store, and define an *Ext.data.proxy.LocalStorage* as follows:

```
Ext.define('NotesApp.store.Notes', {
    extend: 'Ext.data.Store',
    requires: ['Ext.data.proxy.LocalStorage'],
    config: {
        model: 'NotesApp.model.Note',
        proxy: {
            type: 'localstorage',
            id: 'notes-app-store'
        },
        sorters: [{ property: 'dateCreated', direction: 'DESC'}]
    }
});
```

A *LocalStorage* proxy uses the HTML5 *localStorage* API to save model data on the client browser. This proxy is ideal for storing multiple records of similar data. It requires that you provide the *id* config, which is the key that will identify your data in the *localStorage* object.

Now the Notes store has the ability to save and read data from *localStorage*, and you can go back to the NoteEditor view and the controller to take care of the methods that will save the data.

Handling Note Editor events in the controller

In the controller, you are going to use the *control* config to define event handlers for the events fired by the NoteEditor view. You will place these handler declarations under the *noteEditorView ref* that you created earlier in this chapter:

```
control: {
    notesListView: {
        // The commands fired by the notes list container.
```

```
            newNoteCommand: 'onNewNoteCommand',
            editNoteCommand: 'onEditNoteCommand'
    },
    noteEditorView: {
        // The commands fired by the note editor.
        saveNoteCommand: 'onSaveNoteCommand',
        deleteNoteCommand: 'onDeleteNoteCommand',
        backToHomeCommand: 'onBackToHomeCommand'
    }
}
```

Now you can go ahead and implement these handlers. The *onSaveNewNoteCommand* event handler will take care of committing a new or edited note to the Notes store. You will place this handler right after the handlers you previously created in the controller:

```
onSaveNoteCommand: function () {

    console.log('onSaveNoteCommand');

    var noteEditorView = this.getNoteEditorView();
    var currentNote = noteEditorView.getRecord();
    var newValues = noteEditorView.getValues();

    // Update the current note's fields with form values.
    currentNote.set('title', newValues.title);
    currentNote.set('narrative', newValues.narrative);

    var errors = currentNote.validate();

    if (!errors.isValid()) {
        Ext.Msg.alert('Wait!',
errors.getByField('title')[0].getMessage(), Ext.emptyFn);
        currentNote.reject();
        return;
    }

    var notesStore = Ext.getStore('Notes');

    // Is this a new note?
    if (null == notesStore.findRecord('id', currentNote.data.id)) {
        notesStore.add(currentNote);
```

```
    }

    notesStore.sync();

    notesStore.sort([{property: 'dateCreated', direction: 'DESC'}]);

    this.activateNotesList();
},
```

You begin *onSaveNoteCommand* acquiring references to the NoteEditor view, the
note the user is editing, and the values in the form's fields:

```
var noteEditorView = this.getNoteEditorView();
var currentNote = noteEditorView.getRecord();
var newValues = noteEditorView.getValues();
```

Notice how you are using the hidden *getNoteEditorView* method, generated by the
controller based on the *noteEditorView ref*, to reference the NoteEditor view.

Once the refereces are acquired, you transfer the new values from the form
elements to the loaded note:

```
// Update the current note's fields with form values.
currentNote.set('title', newValues.title);
currentNote.set('narrative', newValues.narrative);
```

Model validation in Sencha Touch

Next comes an important part, which is validating the model. To validate the new
values loaded into the model instance, you first call the model's *validate* method,
and then call the *isValid* method on the *Errors* object returned by *validate*:

```
var errors = currentNote.validate();

if (!errors.isValid()) {
    Ext.Msg.alert('Wait!', errors.getByField('title')[0].getMessage(),
Ext.emptyFn);
    currentNote.reject();
```

```
    return;
}
```

The *Ext.data.Model*'s *validate* method iterates over the *validations* defined for the model, and returns an *Ext.data.Errors* instance containing *Ext.data.Error* instances for each model field that is invalid.

In your case, the only field with an attached validator is the note's *title*. When you find that the model is invalid, you first display an alert using the validation's configured *message*, and then call the model's *reject* method, which reverts the modified fields back to their original values. Then, you exit the *onSaveNoteCommand* handler.

Saving notes on the device

After confirming that the modified note is valid, you can move on to save it on the device:

```
var notesStore = Ext.getStore('Notes');

if (null == notesStore.findRecord('id', currentNote.data.id)) {
    notesStore.add(currentNote);
}

notesStore.sync();
```

You use Sencha Touch's helper method *Ext.getStore* to acquire a reference to the Notes store. This method is a shortcut to the *Ext.data.StoreManager.lookup* method, which returns a store registered with the Sencha Touch *StoreManager*.

As *onSaveNoteCommand* works for both new and edited notes, you need to find out if the note is new by searching the store. The store's *findRecord* method helps you try to locate the note. If the note is new, you add it to the store. If the note already exists, you don't need to add it.

The *sync* method asks the store's *proxy* to process all the changes, effectively saving new or edited notes, and removing deleted notes from *localStorage*.

After updating the notes, sort them by date:

```
notesStore.sort([{ property: 'dateCreated', direction: 'DESC'}]);
```

Now that the store is saving its notes to the browser's localStorage, you need to make sure the existing notes are loaded into the store when the Notes app starts. To accomplish this, you are going to quickly jump to the Notes controller and invoke the store's *load* method.

In the controller/Notes.js file, locate the controller's *launch* method, and modify it as follows:

```
launch: function () {
    this.callParent(arguments);
    var notesStore = Ext.getStore('Notes');
    notesStore.load();
    console.log('launch');
},
```

This guarantees that the store is loaded upon Application launch.

Returning to the main view

Our last step in *onSaveNoteCommand* consists of invoking the controller's *activateNotesList* method. This is a helper method, similar to *activateNoteEditor*, which will make the app's NotesList view active:

```
activateNotesList: function () {
    Ext.Viewport.animateActiveItem(this.getNotesListView(),
this.slideRightTransition);
}
```

In this case, you are using a right-slide transition, which you will define in the controller like so:

```
// Transitions
slideLeftTransition: { type: 'slide', direction: 'left' },
slideRightTransition: { type: 'slide', direction: 'right' }
```

What do you think about doing another quick check? This time you should be able to save a note:

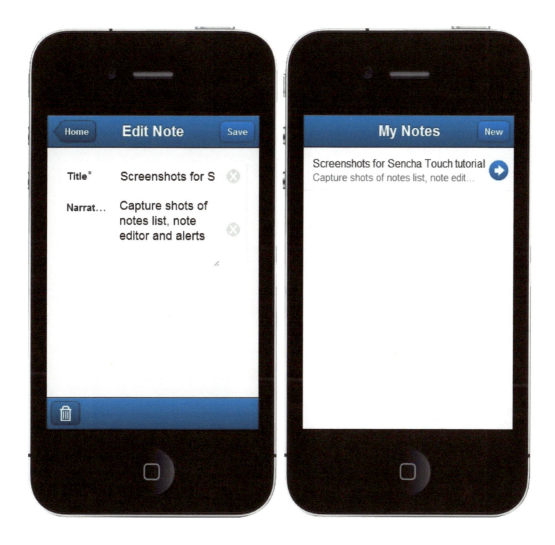

Where are we?

In this chapter you gave your application the ability to save notes on the device. You did so by leveraging the localStorage API, which Sencha Touch exposes through the *LocalStorage* class.

You also practiced how to handle validation errors in a Sencha Touch model, and learned how to add and edit records in a Sencha Touch store.

In the next chapter, you are going to complete the NoteEditor view's features - deleting notes, and canceling edition.

Chapter 6: Deleting Notes

What you will learn in this chapter

The NoteEditor view is missing the ability to delete notes, as well as the ability to cancel editing and return to the NotesList view without making any changes to the selected note. In this chapter you are going to add these features, and finish the application.

The topics you will learn in this chapter are the following:

- How to delete records from a Sencha Touch store.
- How to configure a store so its records are grouped by a given model field.
- How to configure a Sencha Touch List so its items appear grouped.

Deleting notes

The Delete Note workflow begins when a user taps the Delete button, the button with the trash bin icon, on the NoteEditor view:

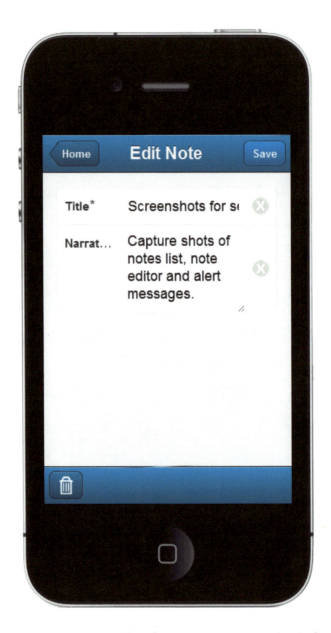

You have already created a *tap* handler for this button, which fires the *deleteNoteCommand* event in the NoteEditor view. The controller executes the *onDeleteNoteCommand* method in response to this event.

In the controller/Notes.js file, you are going to implement the *onDeleteNoteCommand* method as follows:

```
onDeleteNoteCommand: function () {

    console.log('onDeleteNoteCommand');
```

```
    var noteEditorView = this.getNoteEditorView();
    var currentNote = noteEditorView.getRecord();
    var notesStore = Ext.getStore('Notes');

    notesStore.remove(currentNote);
    notesStore.sync();

    this.activateNotesList();
},
```

Your first steps in *onDeleteNoteCommand* consist of acquiring references to the NoteEditor view, the note loaded into the editor, and the Notes store:

```
var noteEditorView = this.getNoteEditorView();
var currentNote = noteEditorView.getRecord();
var notesStore = Ext.getStore('Notes');
```

Next, you proceed to remove the note from the store, and make the changes permanent with a call to the store's *sync* method:

```
notesStore.remove(currentNote);
notesStore.sync();
```

Finally, you activate the app's main view:

```
this.activateNotesList();
```

A quick check with on the app with your favorite WebKit browser should confirm that you are able to delete notes:

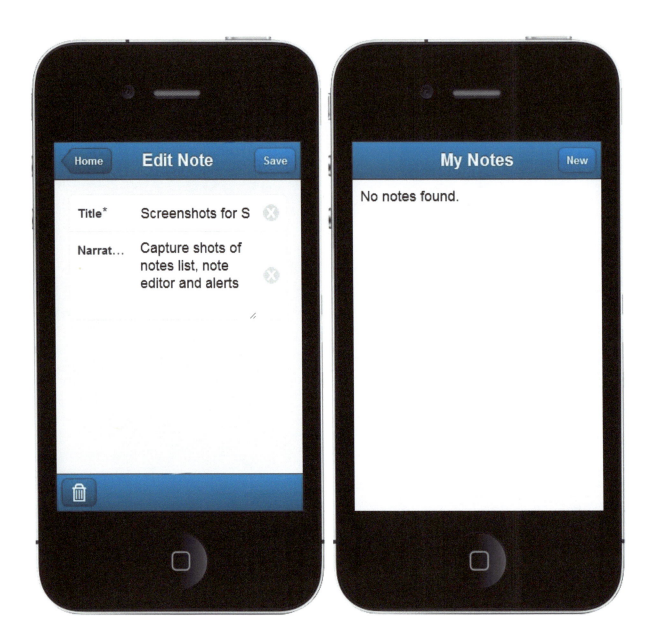

Hooking up the Home button

In order to navigate from the NoteEditor view back to the NotesList view without making any changes to a note, you added a *tap* handler for the Home button in the NoteEditor view. This handler fires the *backToHomeCommand* event from the NoteEditor view. The controller captures this event and binds it to the *onBackToHomeCommand* method.

The *onBackToHomeCommand* method will look like this:

```
onBackToHomeCommand: function () {

    console.log('onBackToHomeCommand');
    this.activateNotesList();
},
```

At this point, you can use your favorite WebKit-powered browser to check that a tap on the Home button activates the NotesList view:

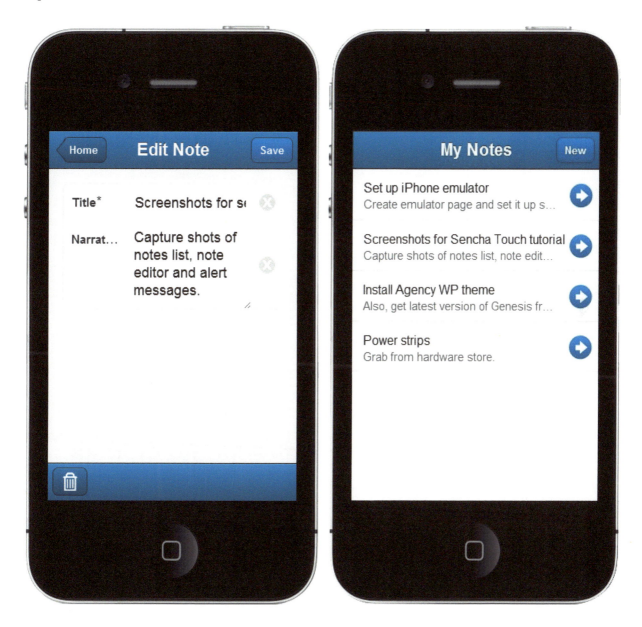

Rendering notes grouped by creation date

One important usability detail that you are missing is the ability to render the cached notes grouped by date.

Let's first jump to the store/Notes.js file and define a *grouper* config for the Notes store:

```
Ext.define('NotesApp.store.Notes', {
    extend: 'Ext.data.Store',
    requires: ['Ext.data.proxy.LocalStorage'],
    config: {
        model: 'NotesApp.model.Note',
        proxy: {
            type: 'localstorage',
            id: 'notes-app-store'
        },
        sorters: [{ property: 'dateCreated', direction: 'DESC'}],
        grouper: {
            sortProperty: 'dateCreated',
            direction: 'DESC',
            groupFn: function (record) {

                if (record && record.data.dateCreated) {
                    return record.data.dateCreated.toDateString();
                } else {
                    return '';
                }
            }
        }
    }
});
```

A grouper's *groupFn* config is the method used to generate the label for the group. In this case, the label will be the creation date of the notes in the group:

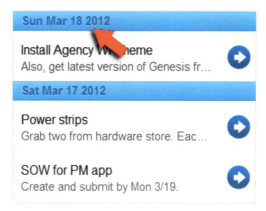

The *sortProperty* config defines the value that you will use to sort the groups. If you do not define a *sortProperty* config, Sencha Touch will sort the groups based on the value returned by the method defined with the *groupFn* config.

The *direction* config specifies the direction to sort the groups.

Over in the view/NotesList.js file, the last change needed to implement grouping consists of adding the *grouped* config to the List component in the NotesList class:

```
{
    xtype: 'list',
    store: 'Notes',
    itemId: 'notesList',
    itemCls: 'list-item-custom',
    loadingText: 'Loading Notes... ',
    emptyText: '<div class="notes-list-empty-text">No notes
found.</div>',
    onItemDisclosure: true,
    grouped: true,
    itemTpl: '<div class="list-item-title">{title}</div><div
class="list-item-narrative">{narrative}</div>'
}
```

When you set the *grouped* config to *true*, the List will use the groups defined in its store, through the store's *grouper* config, to render its items appropriately.

Let's check how the list looks after you turned on grouping. When you start the app with a WebKit browser, the NotesList view will render date groups similar to these:

Where are we?

In this chapter you learned how to delete records from a Sencha Touch store. You also learned how to set up grouping in a store, and how to configure a Sencha Touch List component so its items appear grouped when the List is bound to a grouped store.

You can now move on to the topic of creating a production build of your application. The next chapter will show you how it is done.

Chapter 7: Creating a Production Build

What you will learn in this chapter

In this chapter you will learn how you can use the Sencha Cmd tool to optimize your application for a production deployment. The topics you will explore are the following:

- Installing Sencha Cmd.
- Installing Compass.
- How to use Sencha Cmd to generate an application scaffold, and how to add your application's source code to this scaffold in order to generate a production build.
- How to use Sencha Cmd to create a single compressed JavaScript file containing all the classes used by your application, as well as a single compressed CSS file containing the cascading styles used by your application.

Sencha Cmd is a tool that allows you to perform different tasks related to the creation and deployment of a Sencha Touch and Ext JS applications, from code generation to production builds and native packaging.

You will use Sencha Cmd in a two-step process. First, you will create an application scaffold to which you will add the source code of the Notes app. Then you will generate a production build of the Notes app. This production build will contain an optimized version of the code, images, and other resources, needed by the Notes app to run.

Installing Sencha Cmd

Sencha Cmd is available through the following link:

http://www.sencha.com/products/sencha-cmd/download.

After running the installer, you will open a command line terminal and type in *sencha*, which will produce an output similar to the following screenshot:

```
Sencha Cmd v4.0.0.203
Sencha Cmd provides several categories of commands and some global switches. In
most cases, the first step is to generate an application based on a Sencha SDK
such as Ext JS or Sencha Touch:

    sencha -sdk /path/to/sdk generate app MyApp /path/to/myapp

Sencha Cmd supports Ext JS 4.1.1a and higher and Sencha Touch 2.1 and higher.

To get help on commands use the help command:

    sencha help generate app

For more information on using Sencha Cmd, consult the guides found here:

http://docs.sencha.com/ext-js/4-2/#!/guide/command
http://docs.sencha.com/ext-js/4-1/#!/guide/command

http://docs.sencha.com/touch/2-2/#!/guide/command
http://docs.sencha.com/touch/2-1/#!/guide/command


Options
  * --background, -b - Runs the web server in a background thread
  * --cwd, -cw - Sets the directory from which commands should execute
  * --debug, -d - Sets log level to higher verbosity
  * --nologo, -n - Suppress the initial Sencha Cmd version display
  * --plain, -pl - enables plain logging output (no highlighting)
  * --quiet, -q - Sets log level to warnings and errors only
  * --sdk-path, -s - The location of the SDK to use for non-app commands
  * --time, -ti - Display the execution time after executing all commands

Categories
  * app - Perform various application build processes
  * compass - Wraps execution of compass for sass compilation
  * compile - Compile sources to produce concatenated output and metadata
  * cordova -
  * fs - Utility commands to work with files
  * generate - Generates models, controllers, etc. or an entire application
  * io - Create, deploy and manage applications on the Sencha.io cloud platform
  * iofs - Manage Files stored in the Sencha.io cloud platform
  * manifest - Extract class metadata
  * package - Manages local and remote packages
  * phonegap -
  * repository - Manage local repository and remote repository connections
  * theme - Commands for low-level operations on themes
  * web - Manages a simple HTTP file server

Commands
  * ant - Invoke Ant with helpful properties back to Sencha Cmd
  * build - Builds a project from a legacy JSB3 file.
  * config - Load a properties file or sets a configuration property
  * help - Displays help for commands
  * js - Executes arbitrary JavaScript file(s)
  * upgrade - Upgrades Sencha Cmd
  * which - Displays the path to the current version of Sencha Cmd
```

The output lists the different options available to run Sencha Cmd, and confirms that the installation succeeded.

Installing Compass

Sencha Cmd uses Compass to create application builds; therefore, it is critical that you install Compass before you try to create a build.

The Compass installer is available through the following link: http://compass-style.org/install/.

Once you install Sencha Cmd and Compass, you can proceed to generate an application scaffold that you can use to create a production build of your application.

Creating a scaffold for a production build

The application scaffold will contain all the directories and configuration files needed by Sencha Cmd to produce the production build. Once the scaffold is ready, you will copy the Notes app's source files into its directories, and add the Notes app's information to its build configuration files.

To generate the scaffold, you are going to first go to the command terminal and navigate to the path on your computer that contains the Sencha Touch SDK. For example:

```
cd c:\sencha\touch
```

Then, you will invoke Sencha Cmd's *generate app* command, specifying the path where you want your scaffold created:

```
sencha generate app -path=c:\NotesApp -name NotesApp
```

After the command runs, the *c:\NotesApp* directory will contain the directories depicted in the following screenshot:

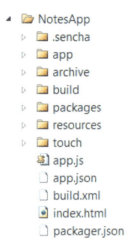

Populating the scaffold with the Notes app's source code

Now you will move the Notes app's source code into the scaffold's directories. You will do so guided by the following steps:

1. Open the Notes app's *resources/css/app.css* file, and copy its contents to the scaffold's *resources/sass/app.scss* file, immediately after the existing content.

2. Open the Notes app's *app.js* file and copy the *name*, *models*, *stores*, *controllers*, and *views* configs, as well as the *launch* function, to the scaffold's *app.js* file. Here you need to be careful not to create duplicate configs, as some of the configs that you are pasting might already exist in the scaffold's *app.js* file.

3. Copy the app's controller file, a*pp/controller/Notes.js*, to the scaffold's *app/controller* directory.

4. Copy the app's model file, *app/model/Note.js*, to the scaffold's *app/model* directory.

5. Copy the app's store file, *app/store/Notes.js* to the scaffold's *app/store* directory.

6. Copy the app's views files, *app/view/NotesList.js* and *app/view/NoteEditor.js*, to the scaffold's *app/view* directory.

7. Delete the *Main.js* file from the scaffold's *app/view* directory. You do not need this view because the app's main view is in the *NotesList.js* file.

8. Open the scaffold's *app.json* file, and set the *name* property as depicted below:

```
/**
    * The application's namespace, used by Sencha Command to
generate classes
    */
"name": "NotesApp",
```

9. Open the scaffold's *.sencha/app/sencha.cfg* file, and set the *app.name* property as depicted below:

```
app.name=NotesApp
```

10. If you are using a Windows PC, give all users Modify permissions to the directory where Sencha Cmd is installed.

At this point, you have updated the scaffold with the application's source, and configured it for a production build. You just need to generate the build.

Generating a production build

To create the production build of the Notes app, you are going to open a command terminal and navigate to the path of the application scaffold you just created:

```
cd c:\NotesApp
```

Then, you are going to execute the *sencha app build* command as follows:

The *sencha app build* command uses the configuration stored in the *app.json* file to create a single compressed JavaScript file that contains the application's JavaScript code and its Sencha Touch dependencies. It also creates a single compressed CSS file that contains the app's styles and its Sencha Touch dependencies.

Sencha Cmd places both files in the *c:\NotesApp\build* directory, where you will also find the images and other resources used by the application:

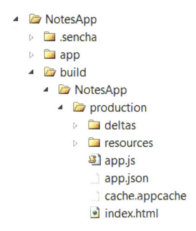

Now you have a build of the Notes app that is suitable for a production deployment. If you load the build's index.html in Chrome and inspect the network requests using Chrome's Developer Tools, you will see that there are fewer requests made to the server and a significant decrease on the number of bytes downloaded, when compared to the development version of the app.

You made it!

I hope this has been a fruitful journey for you. While building the Notes app, you became familiar with the Sencha Touch framework, and learned important practices such as how to capture user input, render data using lists, store information on the device running the application, and build a version of the application suitable for production. This knowledge will definitely help you take the next steps in your path to becoming a great mobile applications developer.

Download the Source Code

You can download a zip file containing the source code for each chapter of the book, as well as the complete application through this link:

http://miamicoder.com/sencha-touch-book-amazon-source-code/

The password for the zip file is *amazon*

Keeping in Touch

Your feedback is very important to me. Please send me your comments or questions through my blog at http://miamicoder.com.

Don't miss my free tutorials, resources, tools and news. Get the best of my work in your inbox for free here: http://miamicoder.com/newsletter-signup/